Wayne

Wayne Dyer Best Quotes and Greatest Life Lessons

Table of contents

Introduction

I want to thank you and congratulate you for downloading the book, *"Wayne Dyer: Wayne Dyer Greatest Life Lessons"*.

Dr. Wayne Dyer is a motivational speaker, spiritual leader and author. His message has been evolving into a more spiritual one and has been greatly influenced by Abraham Maslow's concept of self-actualization and by the teachings of Swami Muktananda.

His first book is called "Your Erroneous Zones" and was an outstanding success which launched his career as a speaker and author.

He has helped millions of people improve the quality of their lives, and in this book I have tried to sum up some of his most important life lessons and philosophies of life, in an attempt to gather the wisdom he is already spreading with his life, books and seminars.

Thanks again for downloading this book, I hope you enjoy it!

Biography

Dyer was born on May 10, 1940 in Detroit, Michigan, to Melvin Lyle and Hazel Irene Dyer and spent much of his childhood, until he was ten years old, in an orphanage on the east side of Detroit.

After graduating from Denby High School, Dyer served in the United States Navy from 1958 to 1962. He received his D.Ed. degree in counseling from Wayne State University for a thesis titled "Group Counseling Leadership Training in Counselor Education"

Dyer worked as a high school guidance counsellor in Detroit and as a professor of counsellor education at St. John's University in New York City. He pursued an academic career, published in journals and established a private therapy practice. His lectures at St. John's, which focused on positive thinking and motivational speaking techniques, attracted many students. A literary agent persuaded Dyer to document his theories in his first book called "Your Erroneous Zones".

Dyer quit his teaching job and began a publicity tour of the United States of America, doggedly pursuing bookstore appearances and media, which eventually led to national television talk show appearances.

Dyer proceeded to build on his success with lecture tours, a series of audiotapes, and regular publication of new books. Dyer's message resonated with many in the New Thought Movement and beyond.

Although Dyer initially resisted the spiritual tag, by the 1990s he had altered his message to include more components of spirituality when he wrote the book "Real Magic", and discussed higher consciousness in the book "Your Sacred Self"

He was influenced by Abraham Maslow's concept of self-actualization and by the teachings of Swami Muktananda whom he considers as his master.

The Power of Thinking and Negative Thoughts

If you would take a deeper and closer look at Dr. Wayne Dyer's works, you can observe that his teachings revolve around the "power of human mind". According to his teachings, your mind is so powerful that it expands and shapes whatever you are harnessing inside; hence, if you harness positive things, then it will define you in a positive way. However, if you gather negative and disempowering thoughts, it is going to manifest clearly in your life. You need to be careful of filling your mind with things that you do not want.

However, despite all the movement that we have seen in positive thinking, why do people always tend to favor negative thoughts to their positive counter parts? As a human being, survival instinct is ingrained in your DNA. There is always that powerful urge to think of a way to get out of a certain bad situation. However, as you try to escape from your predicament, you cannot help but to think of it over and over again. Without you knowing it, instead of harnessing your thoughts and your strength to get away, you become trapped with all the bad things that are happening to you.

Dr. Dyer knows the devastating effects of filling your thoughts with negative things that is why he always includes it in his teachings. He always gives a warning of how your own thinking can stop you from achieving your "perfect, ideal self".

Worrying is normal. It is a basic function of every human. Life is full of problems; make no mistake about that. However, your ability to overcome different trials defines your victory, and not your ability to stick with it. Thinking of your problem over and over again will not help you solve it, thinking of a solution with a positive and healthy mind will.

Many people usually find their deepest source of problem and discouragement from their inability to gain control. Some hate their jobs so much, some hate their bosses, and others hate their low status in society. They define their whole life within the confines of their circumstances. They focus on the negatives, the bad and the ugly; hence, they live within that same sorry state until the day they die even though the reality is they have the power to reverse their fate.

They just could not harness the positive elements in their mind to get them going, to live their lives the way they want it. Remember, what you put in your mind will manifest in your life. If you continue to feed your brain with the things that you do not want, you are going to spend the rest of your life full of agony, regret and discontentment; hence, be careful not to fill your mind with things that you do not want.

Self-worth is what Matters

The very wall that stops people from seeing their true value is their constant desire to win other people's approval and validation. Many are dependent on others to define their own value; hence, they are not seeking for self-worth. They are actually looking for *other-worth*.

If you seek for other people's approval and weigh their opinions more than your own, you are going to have the hardest time finding genuine happiness and contentment. It is because each has a different way of looking at things. They have different ways of perceiving things and not all the time they think of you as someone who matters.

For some, you are the most fabulous and fantastic being. However, for others, you are just nothing. It hurts, and what hurts more is you continuously work on winning them but it is beyond your control.

Stop trying to please everyone. The fact is you can't! Do not ever long for a perfect life when other people set all the criteria. It is like joining a contest where rules are taken away and your chances of winning is never clear. Instead, try to live your life by your own terms. Start pleasing yourself. Start asking for self-validation and start building your self-worth. Not only does it lead you to happy and genuinely contented life. It is also something that you can take full control of.

Living by your terms means you can dictate the desires of your heart without feeling left out and underappreciated by other people. Remember, the only opinion that matters is yours. The only person who can truly appreciate you and see you at your best is yourself. Give yourself a tap on the back whenever you accomplish something. Talk to yourself and tell what a wonderful job you did. Congratulate yourself for your awesomeness. Remind yourself that you are the best and certain trials are just there to make you shine even brighter.

If you appreciate and see yourself for what you are truly worth, then other people will appreciate. If you are truly happy for what you are, then other people can be truly happy to you as well. If you persistently pursue in building your self-worth, others will see you in the best possible way. The real important thing here is you do not care of what they think anymore. All that matters is your own opinion about yourself... and it is beautiful!

Keep Your Ego at Bay; Stay Humble

Have you felt that urgent desire to feel important, to feel special and to feel way above over other people? As a graduate, do you think you have the best education and do you think you deserve that job opening more over the other guy? Do you think you have accomplished so much in life that you deserve better than your peers? If so, maybe your ego is getting the best of you.

When you act based on your ego, there is a great chance that you will be at odds with the world and the people around you. You feel that you are more special than others because of your accomplishments, your education, your work and your possession. Because of that, you are failing to see others' worth and importance. You only act based on what you think, because your opinion is the only one that matters.

You barely admit mistakes; hence, you are depriving yourself of the opportunity to grow because you believe that you got everything you need. You are tarnishing your relationship with others by alienating them with your attitude. Ultimately, you are missing a lot in life!

Dr. Dryer preaches about a life of humility and respect for one's self and others. He always reminds his readers, students and followers to keep their ego at bay and stay humble. He believes in the universal truth that individuals are more common than different with each other; that no one is above someone or more special than others. He believes in the perfect being, the invisible force that created all of us, and so we are one and the same, just performing our own duty in this universe.

Our ego stems from our desire to gain recognition from our achievements and hard work. There is nothing wrong with that. Humans crave to be recognized because it is one of the best feelings in the world. However, when you become overly attached to that idea and your entitlement, that is where ego comes in and it does more bad than good to you.

The best way to be recognized is to stay humble and modest of your accomplishments. Your achievements sound the loudest when you are not telling it to everyone. You can only earn the highest of respect when you give the same amount of respect to others and to yourself. You can only feel truly special when you are not trying to be over someone else's head, but rather carry others on your back to lift them up. That is what matters the most.

Scarcity is Present Only When You Embrace it

What is the difference between successful people and unsuccessful people? Successful people only see opportunity and abundance. Unsuccessful people only see scarcity and despair. Dr. Dyer explains that there is not really a scarcity of opportunity. According to him, opportunities are everywhere, left and right. There is only scarcity in determination and persistence to pursue certain opportunities that come knocking on our doors. What you need to do is to embrace opportunity instead of scarcity.

A lot of people who failed to succeed in life complain that life is unfair and that comforts are only for the privileged ones. It is true that some people were born with a golden spoon and a silver platter. These people never really had to go on a hard days of work. However, it is more of an exception rather than the rule. If you would look at the profile of some of the world's richest people, you will be surprised that majority of them are self-made men and women, who once lived a desperate and sorry life.

The only difference is they never let their circumstance get in the way; instead, they persevere. They worked hard. They never showed fear. They never lose hope and they embrace the opportunity that comes their way. Had Mark Zuckerberg lost hope when he had legal troubles during the early days of Facebook, we would never see Facebook as it is now. Had Steve Jobs elected to put himself in solitary confinement and get stuck in life when he was kicked out from the very company he founded, we would be waiting for so many years before elegant smart phones come in.

As you can see these self-made business titans and successful people are just like every other normal person. They do not possess super powers. They only have super determination to succeed because they embrace opportunity rather than scarcity. They see things in a positive light. There is never a scarcity of determination, only abundance of desire to achieve the goals they set for themselves.

Whenever you feel like nothing is going your way, stop and take a breather. Remember, opportunities are just around you. You need to open both your eyes to see that there is abundance behind the chaos called life. Accept that things will not turn around overnight; but soon, they will if you keep embracing opportunities and working hard to realize it.

Stop Playing the Role of a Victim

When you feel helpless about your situation and you just react instead of respond to it, you are not doing yourself a favor; you are playing the role of a victim. The truth is you are never helpless and hopeless. Just because you are having a big fork on the road does not mean the universe conspired against you. You are the one who is conspiring against yourself to move forward and prosper.

According to Wayne Dyer, the way you react to others and your circumstances is your karma. Meaning, you are accountable and responsible to your thoughts and actions. The moment you start uttering phrases like *"I am tired of this, you are dragging me down, life is not giving me a slack, I don't deserve this treatment, etc."*, you are trying to be helpless and beginning to play the role of a victim. You are looking for someone to rescue you. The truth is nothing is coming for you. The only person who can lift you back on track is none other than yourself.

Everyone is susceptible to this emotional trap. Your boss maybe nagging you; you are about to lose your job; you are experiencing trouble with your marriage; you are getting overdue statements from your bill and credit cards. All these can take a toll on you and it is easy to get trapped and play the role of the victim. Don't!

All you need to do is sit down and take a breather. Do not just react negatively to the situation. Instead, respond with hope and a definite plan to get you out of that swamp. You do not need a "one size fit all solution". All you need are the initial steps to get you going. If you will just focus your energy in resolving your issues rather than focusing on being paralyzed, there is a way out of it!

The most successful people, not only in business but also in life, are the ones who know when to step back and think of their situation. They thrive not because of, but despite their circumstances. They avoid playing the role of a victim because they know they are better than that.

It sounds cliché but the truth is there really is light at the end of the tunnel. However, when you find nothing at all, probably you are not meant to move along. Sometimes, you need to turn back because the right path is the one you just passed a while ago.

On Being Comfortable with your Own Skin

Are you the type of person who is insecure, has low self-esteem, and has no confidence with your own skin? You are not alone. It is surprising to found that the wealthy, the famous and the well to do are some of the most insecure people in the world. You want proof? Look at your boss. If he is the type who keeps losing his cool and trying to control everyone, chances are he is an insecure type. Why? Because he resorts to coercion and other cruel means to run his business or department, instead of trying to just be himself and show his real, caring side.

A person with low self-esteem does not only have a hard time dealing with people. They also lack the sympathy and connection that would make them a warm person. They do not trust their own goodness, that they are capable to be someone who is loved and well respected; hence, they force their authority towards others. They demand respect and admiration instead of earning them. They are missing the warmth of real, genuine relationship.

According to Dr. Wayne Dyer, the loneliest person in the world is the one who is not comfortable to have a lone time with himself. He is not comfortable for who he is, of what he is made of; therefore, he is trying to build a huge wall of himself to the world around him. Sometimes this wall can be translated to rudeness, cruelty, selfishness and lack of warmth and sympathy towards others.

You may be having some troubles or issue with yourself, but do not fall in to this trap. Be the person that you really are. The truth is there is that hidden abundance of warmth, kindness and compassion deep within you. You are just afraid to show it because of fear that people will not appreciate it. Open up and see for yourself what a world of difference it brings to your life when you live confidently. Trust your own goodness. Trust your own kindness.

When you finally unveil that hidden self - that perfect self, people will start to admire and respect you genuinely. People will look at you on a more positive light.

When you finally break that "wall", try to help others break theirs. You may see a lot of rudeness and cruelty from others. Do not take it for what it is. Take it as their cry for help because deep inside, they are struggling. Let your own goodness shine upon them, so that they may finally release themselves from their own shell of insecurity and lack of self-esteem.

Judging Others Negatively Only Harness Resentment

Dr. Wayne Dyer understands the negative impact of judging other people in a negative light. He knows that doing so will not solve the issue. It will not help the person being judged to get better. Instead, you are just encouraging them to be resentful and lose the confidence; hence, he made it a mission through his teachings to free his readers and followers from the need to judge poorly and negatively.

There is a certain satisfaction every time you judge and scold others. Many bosses resort to yelling and humiliating their subordinates when they perform poorly, thinking that they will learn their lessons and do better the next time. A lot of husbands and wives resort to scolding whenever they find something that they dislike about each other. What they do not understand is that it will only harbor resentment. The one being judged, as a default, will only make excuses for his actions instead of admitting it because he does not like to be mistreated.

Try to recall an instance where you scolded, yelled or judged someone in a negative light. What was their reaction? Probably, they were defensive. They had given you all the excuses to justify their actions. They had argued with you and never admitted their mistakes. Now try to remember a time when someone yelled at you or judged you negatively. What was your reaction? Surely, you justified your actions, you argued, and sometimes you went to resent the person who did that to you.

Humans work that way. Humans react that way. It is normal. What many failed to recognize is that we are creatures of emotion not logic; hence, if you scold somebody and tell him that he did something wrong, he will take it personally. He will process it "emotionally" thinking it is not really a way to help him get better. Rather, he would take it as a personal attack to discount him as a person; hence, he will resent you for that.

Dr. Dyer understands this concept well that he encourages everybody to free themselves from the urge to judge anyone in a negative light because when you do, you narrow your vision and only look at the flaws rather than the beauty in someone.

The next time you find any flaws or mistakes from someone, do not be easy to judge. You never know what trials he is passing through. Pull yourself in and think of the negative consequences it might bring to your relationship with that person. If you think that you really need to talk with him, do it in a non-offensive way. Appear as if you are trying to help, that you are a friend not a foe. Ask him if he is having some trouble. Remind him of the consequences that he may have if he continues what he is doing. Let him know that you are there for him.

You Can Only Give What's Inside You

During Dr. Dyer's talk, he would tell his audience to imagine squeezing an orange. He would follow by asking them what comes out when they squeeze the orange. Most of the audience would answer orange juice. Wayne Dyer loves to use this metaphor about squeezing an orange whenever he talks about giving one's self to others.

According to him, you can only give what you have inside you. If you want to cultivate cooperation with your officemates and colleagues to lead a certain project, you need to harness the spirit of cooperation and teamwork within you. If you want to teach your children about respect and responsibility, you need to harbor a certain level of respect and responsibility within you. If you want to give all the love and compassion to your husband or wife, then you need to harbor love and compassion inside you.

Just as you cannot expect an apple or strawberry juice to come out of orange when you squeeze it, you cannot give what you do not have. You cannot effectively teach what you do not practice; therefore, you have to fill yourself with all the things that you want to share with your family, friends and loved ones.

The true beauty of bringing all the good stuff inside you is it radiates towards others. When you do, when your light shines bright, you let others feel good about you and themselves as well. When you foster a healthy relationship with everyone around you by your action, you will lead a happy and fulfilling life. You will start seeing your wife in the most pleasant and attractive way. You will see your kids grow healthy.

You will have stronger bonds with your friends. You will start to have a good working relationship with your boss, your colleagues and customers. You will start enjoying the abundant opportunities that life presented. You will just start experiencing a better life.

No wonder Dr. Wayne Dyer always uses the orange metaphor during his speech and professional engagement. He sees the value and true beauty of it. He understands the powerful impact it gives to every person who harnesses the good and shares it with others. Remember, get all the love, the joy, the peace, confidence, passion and acceptance and share it with others. That way you add up not only to the beauty of your own life but also of others.

Think of Your Goals and Work Backwards to Achieve It

All of us have goals in life. It could be a career goal, a business goal, a goal for your family and your kids, or that personal goal you have been dreaming and working on since you were a kid. It may not seem obvious but humans are truly goal-oriented. They may not always express or imply it, but it is true. It just does not show because most fail in achieving their goals.

The reason why many people fail to achieve their life goals is that once they set it, their vision starts to become clouded along the way. Then, when they start to see some obstacles, they take a step back and reflect on it, thinking that it is too lofty. Hence, they will try to shrink it into a manageable size. Then, they try again. However, because their enthusiasm and passion to reach for it dies down, they start to give up. In the end, nothing is ever accomplished.

The problem with setting a goal is not that you do not have a plan to fulfill it. There is always a plan. You just find it hard to stick with it once your step A does not immediately bring you to step B and so forth. The truth is those predetermined steps do not usually lead you to your desired outcome. It does not always bring you closer to your goals. There will always be variations in results and most of the time, you find yourself going back to your previous steps; hence, you become frustrated. You start to lose your spirit and then you give up.

Many people fall into the same trap and leave their goals unfulfilled. They live their lives full of regrets. Sure, they did their part. It is just that there is something wrong with the way they approached it.

To avoid this common pitfall, try to do things differently. Instead of leading a straight path from A to Z, try to set your goals and envision your steps backward, like from point Z to A.

According to Dr. Wayne Dyer, to have a better success rate in fulfilling your goals, try to determine first your goal then work backwards. Traverse the steps that lead you from your goals to your starting point. That way, you will have complete guidance.

For example, if you are trying to put up your own entrepreneurial venture, determine first your end result. Figure out how you want to be with your business. You can start by determining the monthly income that you are targeting. You can set a figure - say $10,000 per month. Then you have to know how much product you need to sell to reach that milestone. Next, to come up with that sales figure, you need to know the certain group of unique customers that would likely do business with you and buy your stuff, and so on.

This method does not only apply in setting up and achieving your business goals. It is applicable to practically any situation in life.

Never Stop Learning and Be Open to Changes

When do learning stop? Do you stop studying when you finish college or your postgraduate studies? Do you stop acquiring knowledge once you achieve a certain status in society? Probably, you have had enough given the many years you have spent going back and forth in the classroom and library, add the years you spent if you did post grad. However, the things you learned inside the four corners of your classroom are but child's play compared to what you need to prepare yourself in tackling life's challenges and adversities; therefore, no one is exempted to pursue continues education.

Moreover, learning should not be limited to subjects under business or skills. Learning should cover all aspects of life - emotional, personal, financial and spiritual. Dr. Wayne Dyer is not only an advocate of continuous learning and improvement. He also preaches about embracing change, not fearing it. When you obtain fresh knowledge and new ideas, you are now susceptible to change.

The very thing that stops people from learning brand new ways and perspective is their inability to let go of old and obsolete beliefs. Changes follow when you expose yourself to new things. However, when you do not allow yourself to accept and embrace these changes, these new ways, the learning process will not be completed. The benefit of learning is the attraction of abundant opportunities. If you open yourself and absorb knowledge the way a sponge do, you open the doors of opportunities that are once locked outside your system.

However, many people are afraid to learn new things and follow the ways of modern times because they think that it will not do them any better. Moreover, some are just plain lazy to get up and pick the opportunities that learning and change presented. Do not be that kind of person. Do not ever think that achieving a certain milestone is the end of your journey. Remember that you are not only doing it for yourself. You are also doing it for the benefit of the people around you- your family, friends and loved ones.

If you want to see a dramatic change in your life, do not get stuck inside your room watching television the whole day. Go out once in a while. Meet your old friends. Talk with them and learn a thing or two from their experiences. Find yourself a mentor, someone who has already walked the same path you are walking right now.

Ask for some advice, some guidance and steps that you could follow. Learn about their mistakes so you can avoid them. It is not difficult to find one. A lot of potential mentors would be more than glad to help you because it is part of their own self-fulfillment. Enroll to some available classes in your community. You will never know what opportunities might come.

Do not Back Down from Rejection

One of the worst feelings in the world is getting rejected by someone. When you receive rejection, it hurts deep inside. It is humiliating. It shatters your confidence and self-esteem. When you get rejected over and over again, it encourages you to build a wall for yourself so that you will avoid being rejected again because it is such a bad experience.

Do you know why dating applications like Tinder are so popular? It is because of their deep understanding of that very sensitive human emotion, the feeling of rejection. Normally, a guy or a lady would go out, probably in a bar or some public places, to meet new people. With Tinder, you no longer need to go out, introduce yourself, carry a couple of punch lines and risk being rejected. Everything can be done at a single swipe on your smart phone and you would instantly know if somebody likes you. You won't ever know if somebody dislikes you. You avoid the risk of being rejected and hurt.

These kinds of smart phone applications are so useful that millions of people are using it. In fact, if a technology would be created to apply the same principle of Tinder to other confrontational activities like selling, business proposal, among others, it will be popular as well. However, this kind of mentality and view towards rejection is not healthy. It takes away your ability to persist, to be creative, to learn and to be as human as possible.

Rejection maybe truly hurtful but it is not bad for you. In fact, being rejected is healthy if you can handle it well. You just need to learn not to take it on a personal level. You just have to embrace the concept in a positive light. Take it as a normal occurrence because the truth is not everyone is persuadable, not everyone is sellable. Understand that you can only sell products, beliefs and ideas to people who need them.

If you chance upon the wrong person, then you can always move on until you find someone. Remember, being rejected is not a product of your own shortcomings; it is just a circumstance of life, that the person you come across is not sold to you.

Do not take rejection as something to be ashamed of. Do not be afraid to look foolish to everyone. Sometimes, you need to look foolish in the name of achieving progress. How many times have you heard of a story where a certain job applicant walked in to as many offices in his city and no one ever took him? Turns out he tried his luck in business and became very successful with it!

Never let rejection knock you down. Just keep going, keep pushing then thank everyone who snubbed you. It is because of them that you gained the courage to do it all by yourself.

Do What You Truly Love and Fulfill Your Real Destiny

Do you want to know what your real destiny is? It is to live a life of happiness and abundance, regardless of its sources. You might probably say, "Yeah right!" but that is the truth. We are all meant to spend a life of happiness and abundance with people who matter to us, the ones we love. However, only a few people can fulfill this destiny. In fact, many rich and successful people claim that they have yet to discover their destiny, their life of happiness and abundance despite their status.

The reason why a lot of people failed to find their destiny and treat it as if it is a Holy Grail is because they forget the fundamental idea that they need to learn to fulfill it - *clearly defining the things that make you happy.* If you do not know what makes you happy, just living your life so you could gain acceptance and validation from others, working so hard to gain vast amount of wealth and thinking that it is the ultimate source of happiness, then you are going to live the rest of your life in despair and discontentment.

The secret to a fulfilling life is doing every day the things that you enjoy the most. If you are happy with what you do you, with what you have and with who you are, you will never feel incomplete. Another thing is to surround yourself with people whom you love and love you back. Also, spend your time with likeminded people who share the same idea and vision of a perfect life. When you are surrounded with people who matter to you and understand you deeply, you will never have to pretend. You can be your most genuine and perfect self and everyone will appreciate you for that.

In the end, it is not about how much money you earn because it cannot buy you genuine happiness. You do not need to be associated with famous and well to do people so you'd feel good about yourself. You do not need to possess all the things in the world; you don't need all of them. You just have to work hard with dogged resolve to find your destiny and realize it, and your destiny is always to live a happy and fulfilling life.

13

Do not Just Live for Others, Live for Yourself

Do you usually find yourself making a comparison between your accomplishment and your Facebook friends'? Are you fired up and motivated to get a brand new luxury car because your neighbor next door just got himself a shiny one? Do you work so hard to get that promotion so you could finally overtake your best friend's accomplishments? If you are living that kind of life, then you are not living it for yourself. You are living it for others.

According to Dr. Wayne Dyer, when you are trying to outdo just about everyone you know, when you are always in a rush to overtake someone else's achievement, you are giving up your unique gift to be in control. Instead, you are giving the other person the power to control you. When you are always comparing yourself with others, you discount your own achievements. You would always think of yourself as "not good enough" and the cycle never ends.

It is good to appreciate and recognize other's self-entitlement. When you are always in competition against your colleagues, you will have the tendency to get your vision clouded and think for your own benefit and not the company's. When that happens, you will only do yourself more harm than pleasure. Instead of trying to be competitive with everyone, try to be cooperative. Work harmoniously with your colleagues. Exchange ideas and knowledge with your friends. Gain from everyone and let everyone gain from you. Define your own version of success. Take control of your life. Coexist!

Remember, you are not answerable to anyone but only to the person you spend time with when you are alone- yourself! Do not let others dictate how you would live your life by trying to be overly competitive with them. Get the competition to a healthy level. Think of your successful friends and colleagues as inspiration rather than competition. When you are inspired, you are not pushing yourself to a level that is destructive and dangerous. Instead, you are working on because you understand what is really good for you.

Always Be Grateful

Lastly, one of the best yet very simple teachings of Dr. Wayne Dyer is to be always in awe of all the good things that you attracted in your life, whether it is love, family, career, wealth or health. He gives emphasis on showing gratitude at all times. Because according to him, when you are being grateful, when you are feeling thankful of all the wealth and abundance you are experiencing, you are opening a bigger door to invite more opportunities in life.

If you are grateful of what you have whether small or big things, happiness will not escape you. It will linger to you. The secret to life of contentment is that simple. For example, if you are living in a small house, instead of complaining, you could choose to be thankful that you have a roof that protects, that keeps you safe. Remember, you are always in control of your emotion. There are outside forces that affect you, but in the end, it is still up to you. You always have the choice to be happy with what you have and be thankful for it.

The next time you wake up in the morning, sit back and thank the powerful forces that keep you alive and free from any danger or defects. You can still be grateful even if things do not go your way. The key here is not to focus with your problems but focus on the good side that your problem brings. For example, if you have just let your work go, it is okay to be scared. Just do not let it cripple you. Think of it as a chance to grab the better opportunity that waits you, opportunities that you cannot get from your dead end job.

That is what Wayne Dyer is pointing out that when you are

grateful despite your situation, you are attracting that invisible power to bring you abundance in life.

Wayne Dyer's Best Quotes

"How people treat you is their karma; how you react
is yours."

Wayne W. Dyer

"Change the way you look at things and the things you
look at change."

Wayne W. Dyer

"Friends are God's way of apologizing for your
family."

Wayne W. Dyer

"With everything that has happened to you, you can
either feel sorry for yourself or treat what has
happened as a gift. Everything is either an
opportunity to grow or an obstacle to keep you from
growing. You get to choose."

Wayne W. Dyer

"When you judge another, you do not define them,
you define yourself."

Wayne W. Dyer

"You cannot be lonely if you like the person you're alone with."

Wayne W. Dyer

"You are not stuck where you are unless you decide to be."

Wayne W. Dyer

"Passion is a feeling that tells you: this is the right thing to do. Nothing can stand in my way. It doesn't matter what anyone else says. This feeling is so good that it cannot be ignored. I'm going to follow my bliss and act upon this glorious sensation of joy."

Wayne W. Dyer

"All blame is a waste of time. No matter how much fault you find with another, and regardless of how much you blame him, it will not change you. The only thing blame does is to keep the focus off you when you are looking for external reasons to explain your unhappiness or frustration. You may succeed in making another feel guilty about something by blaming him, but you won't succeed in changing whatever it is about you that is making you unhappy."

"Your reputation is in the hands of others. That's what the reputation is. You can't control that. The only thing you can control is your character."

Wayne W. Dyer

"When the choice is to be right or to be kind, always make the choice that brings peace"

Wayne W. Dyer

"I am realistic – I expect miracles."

Wayne W. Dyer

"You have everything you need for complete peace and total happiness right now."

Wayne W. Dyer

"The more you see yourself as what you'd like to become, and act as if what you want is already there, the more you'll activate those dormant forces that will collaborate to transform your dream into your reality."

Wayne W. Dyer

"Conflict cannot survive without your participation"

Wayne W. Dyer

"Circumstances do not make a man, they reveal him."

Wayne W. Dyer

"You'll see it when you believe it."

Wayne W. Dyer

"If you knew who walked beside you at all times, on the path that you have chosen, you could never experience fear or doubt again."

Wayne W. Dyer

"Heaven on Earth is a choice you must make, not a place you must find."

Wayne W. Dyer

"you don't need to be better than anyone else you just need to be better than you used to be"

Wayne W. Dyer

"Begin to see yourself as a soul with a body rather than a body with a soul."

Wayne W. Dyer

"In any relationship in which two people become one, the end result is two half people."

Wayne W. Dyer

"Your children will see what you're all about by what you live rather than what you say."

Wayne W. Dyer

"Loving people live in a loving world; hostile people live in a hostile world; same world."

Wayne W. Dyer

"When you dance, your purpose is not to get to a certain place on the floor. It's to enjoy each step along the way."

Wayne W. Dyer

"You cannot always control what goes on outside. But you can always control what goes on inside."

"We are not human beings in search of a spiritual experience. We are spiritual beings emersed in a human experience."

Wayne W. Dyer

"Each experience in your life was absolutely necessary in order to have gotten you to the next place, and the next place, up to this very moment."

Wayne W. Dyer

"Be miserable. Or motivate yourself. Whatever has to be done, it's always your choice."

Wayne W. Dyer

"When you're at peace with yourself and love yourself, it is virtually impossible to do things to yourself that are destructive."

Wayne W. Dyer

"Before speaking, consult your inner-truth barometer, and resist the temptation to tell people only what they want to hear."

"I would rather be hated for who I am than loved for whom I'm not."

"Go for it now. The future is promised to no one."

"The highest form of ignorance is when you reject something you don't know anything about"

"I am thankful to all those who said no. It's because of them, I did it myself."

"There's no scarcity of opportunity to make a living at what you love. There is only a scarcity of resolve to make it happen."

"Make peace with silence, and remind yourself that it

is in this space that you'll come to remember your spirit. When you're able to transcend an aversion to silence, you'll also transcend many other miseries. And it is in this silence that the remembrance of God will be activated."

Wayne W. Dyer

"You leave old habits behind by starting out with the thought, 'I release the need for this in my life'."

Wayne W. Dyer

"The state of your life is nothing more than a reflection of the state of your mind."

Wayne W. Dyer

"You are in a partnership with all other human beings, not a contest to be judged better than some and worse than others."

Wayne W. Dyer

"You'll seldom experience regret for anything that you've done. It is what you haven't done that will torment you. The message, therefore, is clear. Do it! Develop an appreciation for the present moment. Seize every second of your life and savor it."

"What comes out of you when you are squeezed is what is inside of you."

"Doing what you love is the cornerstone of having abundance in your life."

"When you are able to shift your inner awareness to how you can serve others, and when you make this the central focus of your life, you will then be in a position to know true miracles in your progress toward prosperity."

"If we focus on what's ugly, we attract more ugliness into our thoughts, and then into our emotions, and ultimately into our lives"

"When you abandon making choices, you enter the vast world of excuses."

"It is easy to love people when they smell good, but sometimes they slip into the manure of life and smell awful. You must love them just as much when they smell foul."

Wayne W. Dyer

"All blame is a waste of time. No matter how much fault you find with another, it will not change you."

Wayne W. Dyer

"It's never crowded along the extra mile"

Wayne W. Dyer

"Everything I need now is here"

Wayne W. Dyer

"Present-moment living, getting in touch with your now, is at the heart of effective living. When you think about it, there really is no other moment you can live. Now is all there is, and the future is just another present moment to live when it arrives."

Wayne W. Dyer

"You get treated in life the way you teach people to treat you."

Wayne W. Dyer

"Peace is the result of retraining your mind to process life as it is, rather than as you think it should be."

Wayne W. Dyer

"You are what you choose to be today. Not what you've chosen to be before."

Wayne W. Dyer

"Don't die with the music still in you."

Wayne W. Dyer

"Once you believe in yourself and see your soul as divine and precious, you'll automatically be converted to a being who can create miracles."

Wayne W. Dyer

"Embrace silence since meditation is the only way to

truly come to know your Source."

Wayne W. Dyer

"Begin with the end in mind. Start with the end outcome and work backwards to make your dream possible."

Wayne W. Dyer

"A mind at peace a mind centered and not focused on harming others is stronger than any physical force in the universe."

Wayne W. Dyer

"No one knows enough to be a pessimist."

Wayne W. Dyer

"As You Think, So Shall You Be."

Wayne W. Dyer

"I have absolutely no limits on what I intent to create."

Wayne W. Dyer

"If you meet someone whose soul is not aligned with yours, send them love and move along."

Wayne W. Dyer

"Never underestimate your power to change yourself; never overestimate your power to change others."

Wayne W. Dyer

"Love what you do; Do what you love."

Wayne W. Dyer

"Not only do you become what you think about, but the world also becomes what you think about. Those who think that the world is a dark place are blind to the light that might illuminate their lives. Those who see the light of the world view the dark spots as merely potential light."

Wayne W. Dyer

"You are an infinite spiritual being having a temporary human experience."

Wayne W. Dyer

"The meaning of life is to get meaning for life."

"The purpose of dancing isn't to end up at a particular spot on the floor. The purpose of dancing and of life is to enjoy every moment and every step, regardless of where you are when the music ends."

Wayne W. Dyer

"No one can create negativity or stress within you. Only you can do that by virtue of how you process your world."

Wayne W. Dyer

"Attachment to being right creates suffering. When you have a choice to be right, or to be kind, choose kind and watch your suffering disappear."

Wayne W. Dyer

"Love is the ability and willingness to allow those that you care for to be what they choose for themselves without any insistence that they satisfy you."

Wayne W. Dyer

"Your teacher might be a child who takes you by the

hand and asks you a question that you hadn't considered before, and your answer to the child is your answer to yourself."

Wayne W. Dyer

"You must become the producer, director and actor in the unfolding story of your life."

Wayne W. Dyer

"Everything in the universe has a purpose. Indeed, the invisible intelligence that flows through everything in a purposeful fashion is also flowing through you"

Wayne W. Dyer

"What we think determines what happens to us, so if we want to change our lives, we need to stretch our minds."

Wayne W. Dyer

"Enjoying life is far superior to being graded on your performance in life."

Wayne W. Dyer

"We are divine enough to ask and we are important enough to receive."

Wayne W. Dyer

"You cannot fail, you can only produce results."

Wayne W. Dyer

"A non-doer is very often a critic-that is, someone who sits back and watches doers, and then waxes philosophically about how the doers are doing. It's easy to be a critic, but being a doer requires effort, risk, and change."

Wayne W. Dyer

"There is one grand lie - that we are limited. The only limits we have are the limits we believe."

Wayne W. Dyer

"A belief system is nothing more than a thought you've thought over and over again."

Wayne W. Dyer

"Society demands conformity at the expense of

to be fully alive."

Wayne W. Dyer

"The last suit that you wear, you don't need any
pockets."

Wayne W. Dyer

"Remind yourself that you cannot fail at being
yourself."

Wayne W. Dyer

"Love is my gift to the world. I fill myself with love,
and I send that love out into the world."

Wayne W. Dyer

"My goal is not to be better than anyone else, but to
be better than I used to be."

Wayne W. Dyer

"The greatest gift that you were ever given was the gift
of your imagination."

Wayne W. Dyer

"Remember, purpose is about giving...All you can do with your life is to give it away in the service of others."

Wayne W. Dyer

"An infinity of forest lies dormant within the dreams on one acorn."

Wayne W. Dyer

"Acceptance means no complaining, and happiness means no complaining about the things over which you can do nothing."

Wayne W. Dyer

"When you squeeze an orange, you'll always get orange juice to come out. What comes out is what's inside. The same logic applies to you: when someone squeezes you, puts pressure on you, or says something unflattering or critical, and out of you comes anger, hatred, bitterness, tension, depression, or anxiety that is what's inside. If love and joy are what you want to give and receive, change your life by changing what's inside."

Wayne W. Dyer

"Judgements prevent us from seeing the good that lies beyond appearances."

Wayne W. Dyer

"The words I AM are your sacred identification as God- your highest self. Take care how you use this terms because saying anything after I AM that's incongruent with God is really taking the Lord's name in vain!"

Wayne W. Dyer

"I think and that is all that I am."

Wayne W. Dyer

"Becoming the observer (step back) you begin to live in process, trusting where our source is taking you. You begin to detach from the outcome. That detachment allows you to stop fighting and allows things to just come to you; you no longer make things happen but allow them to show up. The fight is gone!"

Wayne W. Dyer

"Banish doubt. When doubt is banished, abundance flourishes and anything is possible."

Wayne W. Dyer

"You are always a valuable, worthwhile human being -
- not because anybody says so, not because you're
successful, not because you make a lot of money -- but
because you decide to believe it and for no other
reason."

Wayne W. Dyer

"When you change the way you look at things, the
things you look at change."

Wayne W. Dyer

"The antidote to fear is faith."

"When you have a choice to be right, or to be kind,
choose to be kind."

Wayne W. Dyer

"Freedom means you are unobstructed in living your
life as you choose. Anything less is a form of slavery."

Wayne W. Dyer

"Self-worth comes from one thing, thinking that you
are worthy."

"Real magic in relationships means an absence of judgment of others."

Wayne W. Dyer

"Live one day at a time emphasizing ethics rather than rules."

Wayne W. Dyer

"It makes no sense to worry about things you have no control over because there's nothing you can do about them, and why worry about things you do control? The activity of worrying keeps you immobilized."

Wayne W. Dyer

"It is impossible for you to be angry and laugh at the same time. Anger and laughter are mutually exclusive and you have the power to choose either."

Wayne W. Dyer

"Miracles come in moments. Be ready and willing."

Wayne W. Dyer

"When you squeeze an orange, orange juice comes out, because that's what's inside. When you are squeezed, what comes out is what is inside."

Wayne W. Dyer

"When I chased after money, I never had enough. When I got my life on purpose and focused on giving of myself and everything that arrived into my life, then I was prosperous."

Wayne W. Dyer

"Transformation literally means going beyond your form."

Wayne W. Dyer

"Our intention creates our reality."

Wayne W. Dyer

"See the light in others, and treat them as if that is all you see."

Wayne W. Dyer

"Honor the physical temple that houses you by eating

and treating it with dignity and love."

"You create your thoughts, your thoughts create your intentions and your intentions create your reality."

"Every time I pick up a coin on the street, I view it as a symbol of the abundance that God sends into my life, and feel gratitude. "Thank you, God, for everything" Never do I ask, "Why only a penny?"."

"Find a favorite little something in every day."

"The more we give away, the more is given to us."

"As I unclutter my life, I free myself to answer the callings of my soul."

"The more you extend kindness to yourself, the more it will become your automatic response to others."

Wayne W. Dyer

"Anytime you start a sentence with I AM, you are creating what you are and what you want to be."

Wayne W. Dyer

"The only difference between a flower and a weed is judgment."

Wayne W. Dyer

"Abundance is not something we acquire. It's something we tune into."

Wayne W. Dyer

"If you are living out of a sense of obligation you are a slave."

Wayne W. Dyer

"There is a secret garden where miracles and magic abound, and it's available to anyone who makes the choice to visit there."

"Remember that your natural state is joy."

"Anything that immobilizes you, gets in your way or keeps you from your goals is all yours. You can throw it away anytime you choose."

"Keep reminding yourself: I get what I think about, whether I want it or not."

"You don't have to see the whole staircase, just take the first step."

"Let the world know why you're here, and do it with passion."

"You are a Divine creation, a being of light, who

showed up here as a human being at the exact moment you were supposed to. You are the beloved, a miracle, a part of the eternal perfection."

Wayne W. Dyer

"You do not attract what you want. You attract what you are."

Wayne W. Dyer

"Everything that shows up in your life is supposed to. This includes the falls in your life, which provide you with the energy to propel yourself to a higher state of awareness."

Wayne W. Dyer

"If you correct your mind, your life will follow."

Wayne W. Dyer

"You can feel purposeful every single day by taking a moment to cheer up a disgruntled employee, make a child laugh, or even pick up a piece of litter and place it in a trash can."

Wayne W. Dyer

"There is a spiritual solution to every problem."

Wayne W. Dyer

"Attitude is everything so pick a good one."

Wayne W. Dyer

"The measure of your life will not be in what you accumulate but in what you give away."

Wayne W. Dyer

"There is no stress in the world, only people thinking stressful thoughts and then acting on them."

Wayne W. Dyer

"I match my thoughts to what I want."

Wayne W. Dyer

"Gratitude is absolutely the way to bring more into your life."

Wayne W. Dyer

"There's nothing wrong with anger provided you use

it constructively."

Wayne W. Dyer

Conclusion

Thank you again for downloading this book!

I hope this book was able to give you the possibility to see life with new light and find new ideas and resources to improve some aspects of your life.

Sometimes we face very challenging and difficult situations or just things aren't the way we want, but we always have the power to change ourselves and transform our lives.

It is not what happens that determines the quality of our lives, but what we do with what happens.

Thank you and good luck!

Preview Of 'Eckhart Tolle: Eckhart Tolle Best Quotes and Greatest Life Lessons'

I want to thank you and congratulate you for downloading the book, *"Eckhart Tolle: Eckhart Tolle Greatest Life Lessons"*.

Eckhart Tolle is a spiritual teacher and author who was born in Germany and educated at the Universities of London and Cambridge.

His first book, "The Power of Now", has been more than 100 times in the New York Times Best Sellers list. This book and its second part "A New Earth" are considered to be some of the most influential spiritual books in the world nowadays.

Eckhart's profound yet simple teachings have already helped countless people throughout the world find inner peace and greater fulfillment in their lives. At the core of the teachings lies the transformation of consciousness, a spiritual awakening that he sees as the next step in human evolution. An essential aspect of this awakening consists in transcending our ego-based state of consciousness. This is a prerequisite not only for personal happiness but also for the ending of violence on our planet.

In this book I have tried to sum up some of his most important life lessons and philosophies of life, in an attempt to gather the wisdom he is already spreading with his life, books and seminars.

Thanks again for downloading this book, I hope you enjoy it!

Biography

Eckhart Tolle was born Ulrich Leonard Tölle in Lünen, a small town located north of Dortmun (Germany), in 1948. Tolle describes his childhood as unhappy, particularly his early childhood in Germany. His parents eventually separated, and he felt alienated from a hostile school environment. At the age of 13, he moved to Spain to live with his father. Tolle's father did not insist that his son attend high school, so Tolle elected to study literature, astronomy and languages at home.

At the age of 15 Tolle read several books written by the German mystic Joseph Anton Schneiderfranken.

At the age of 19, Tolle moved to England and for three years taught German and Spanish at a London school for language studies. Troubled by "depression, anxiety and fear", he began "searching for answers" in his life.

At age 22 or so, he decided to pursue this search by studying philosophy, psychology, and literature, and enrolled in the University of London. After graduating, he was offered a scholarship to do postgraduate research at Cambridge University which he began in 1977 and from which he dropped out soon after.

One night in 1977, at the age of 29, after having suffered from long periods of suicidal depression, Tolle says he experienced an "inner transformation". That night he awakened from his sleep, suffering from feelings of depression that were "almost unbearable," but then experienced a life-changing epiphany. Recounting the experience, Tolle says:

I couldn't live with myself any longer. And in this a question arose without an answer: who is the 'I' that cannot live with the self? What is the self? I felt drawn into a void! I didn't know at the time that what really happened was the mind-made self, with its heaviness, its problems, that lives between the unsatisfying past and the fearful future, collapsed. It dissolved. The next morning I woke up and everything was so peaceful. The peace was there because there was no self, just a sense of presence or "beingness," just observing and watching.

Tolle recalls going out for a walk in London the next morning, and finding that "everything was miraculous, deeply peaceful. The feeling continued, and he began to feel a strong underlying sense of peace in any situation. Tolle stopped studying for his doctorate, and for a period of about two years after this he spent much of his time sitting, "in a state of deep bliss," on park benches in Russell Square, Central London, "watching the world go by". His family thought him irresponsible, even insane.

Tolle's first book, "The Power of Now", was first published in 1997 by Namaste Publishing. Only 3000 copies were published of the first edition. In 2000 Oprah Winfrey recommended it in her magazine. In August 2000 it reached the New York Times Best Seller list for Hardcover Advice. After two more years, it was number one on that list. The book had been translated from English into 33 languages.

In 2003 he published his second book, "Stillness Speaks", and in 2005 he launched his third book, "A New Earth".

Do Not Define Your Life According to What or How Much You Own

There are plenty of people who live miserably for the better part of their lives. Some may live with all the comforts money can buy, but even with a thick wallet and fat bank account, they are still miserable.

Others make it seem like they are having the time of their lives leading successful careers. They do what others can only dream of. However, none of it matters if it is not where your heart truly is. All the money in the world won't be enough make you happy.

A chest of gold can't buy inner peace. You can be king or queen and still dislike yourself or still live in misery. On the other hand, you can live a simple life and live happily. You may not be the most popular, the richest, or the most adored but the most important thing is that you are pleased with yourself. That is how you find happiness and peace. That is what you can call success.

Eckhart Tolle offers us one of the most valuable lessons in life that so many people disregard. It is that life is not about the money—it never really is. It is not about how much you own or what. You can earn six figures a month and still feel unhappy. You can be swimming in dollar bills and still feel empty inside. The simple truth is money does not equate to success. Money alone cannot bring you happiness.

Money may allow you to afford material things. It may even buy you some privilege. With enough money, you may even get power but that is all. The most important things in life cannot be bought by money.

Money is essential but it is not the most important.

We do need to be practical. Let's not be hypocrites and say we do not need money. We need money to survive. Having money can help us live comfortably. To a certain extent, money with all the things it can afford can bring us some joy. If you are looking for the real thing, however, you should not be relying on money for answers.

Money is practical. It can free you from worrying about material needs. It is not, however, the answer to all your needs. You should never make money or the desire for material possessions a guide for making decisions in your life.

So how will you define success and happiness then?

You will find success and happiness when you find your purpose, when you pursue the things you genuinely enjoy doing. The question is: are you doing what you really want right now? Are you pursuing the career path you have always dreamed of? How will you know? Ask the following questions.

- Am I at peace with myself?

- Am I confident?

- Am I energetic?

- Do I look forward to going to work every single day?

- Am I content?

- Am I enthusiastic?

- Can I think of anything else I'd rather be doing?

Is it time to move on? Here are some of the common signs that it is time to re-think your career choice.

Your body is aching

When you feel rotten inside, it will also manifest as physical pain. If you are always exhausted and have trouble concentrating, it may be a better idea to ditch your current job. There is what they call Sunday-night dread. It happens to people who hate Mondays because they feel they are about to jump into a bottomless pit again.

If you experience muscle tension, headaches, and migraines, consider these as signs you are pursuing the wrong career. It does not get any better if you stay on it longer.

Work-related stress can affect your physical well being. Soon enough, your mental health will suffer as well. It does not just affect you. It also consumes the people around you.

Stress has become your nickname

Surely, we all have something to complain about especially when it comes to our jobs. We all get tired and worn out but it is an entirely different matter if you are always stressed out. Are you constantly complaining? Do you feel unhappy about your job? Do you still remember how it feels like to be excited and inspired? Or does it feel like ages ago since the last time you felt that way?

When you rarely have the time or you are completely lacking in energy doing the things that you used to, you must reconsider your options. If you hardly spend time with your family and friends and on rare occasions that you are present, you're too stressed out to enjoy their company, then you should take it as a clear warning sign.

If your job has turned you into a person your family and friends do not recognize anymore or if you have become this person you do not like, then consider for a minute that this job may not be the right one for you.

You feel bad about yourself

We all dream of fulfilling careers. That's where we find confidence. On the other hand, if you feel like your job is taking a toll on your emotional well being, it is never a good sign.

If you have become less confident in your decision making abilities, it may not be your fault. It will be however, if you continue on the career path that is just not meant for you. If you have become stagnant, if you do not see any opportunity for growth or if you feel like it is impossible to complete a single simple task, you need to make a dramatic change.

The only thing that's making you stay is the money

Will you stay in a job that pays a lot but makes you feel miserable? Will you stay even if it feels like a nightmare? The truth is money cannot accomplish anything but buy you material comforts that meet your physical needs. If you seriously want to find deeper meaning, a sense of purpose and true success and happiness, you need to set aside the thought of money for a second. The truth is no amount of money is worth sacrificing your health and happiness for.

may be envied by your friends. You may have a castle like house or fancy cars. None of it can fill up the hole that eats you up inside. It is simply not worth it. Deep inside, you know it too.

You are bored

Enthusiasm and energy put you at the top of your game. You lack energy and enthusiasm and it is hard to put yourself in that state when you simply do not enjoy your job. If you have to drag yourself out of bed to go to work, you need to start shaking things up. Although no one can sustain great fascination every single morning of every day on the job, it only gets much more difficult for someone who does not genuinely enjoy their line of work.

Your life lacks balance

Do you spend more time at work than at home? Whenever you're at home, are you constantly worried about work? It only means one thing. Work-life balance is non-existent.

You are underappreciated

If your skills are not tapped into or you are simply not appreciated for the things you bring to the table, you seriously need to move on. Start looking for a new and better opportunity, one that helps you in realizing your full potential.

You dream about doing something else

If you can think of anything you'd rather be doing than sitting on your fancy desk in your corner office, it is a clear sign to move on. You will feel more heart sick when you do nothing about what your instincts are telling you.

You've given up

Your ideas were shot down many times before and it does not seem like you will be promoted any time soon so you have given up all hope. You are no longer actively seeking opportunities for advancement within the company. You are satisfied with coasting along. This is the exact opposite of a fulfilling career.

You will leave if you get the chance

Perhaps it is about the money. You may be thinking you are being practical about it. If you lose this job then you will lose a source of income. That's the only thing that's keeping you in the job. You are hanging by a thin thread. You simply cannot take it anymore.

Change can be scary. It entails uncertainty. Change is never safe. There is always a risk. Will you continue to fear change? Will you always stay safe? If you choose to stay within your comfort zone, you may be safe and you may never fall backwards but you will never move forward either. You will never go as far as you could possibly imagine. You remain stagnant.

How do you make a change?

If you do decide to take the first steps to a big change, you can use the following tips as a guide.

Decide what to do next

Now is the time to think about what to do and where to go next. You have to make a decision. Figure out the path you want to take.

What is it that makes you happy doing? What do you enjoy spending time and energy on? What line of work can help you cultivate your strengths and channel your weaknesses properly?

Develop your skills

Once you have decided on which route to take, you have to prepare yourself by upgrading your skill set. It is important to have the right attitude and the proper set of skills to launch you forward. This is how you can mold your career into something worthwhile.

There are people who know what they want to do with their lives at an early age. Age does not matter here as long as you figure it out. When you finally do, you must make the effort to prepare yourself. When you spend time improving your craft, your efforts will eventually pay off.

Find a mentor

A mentor can provide exactly what you need to make your dream career a reality. Your mentor can provide unwarranted support as well as offer an invaluable resource to guide you in whatever direction you wish to take.

Build your network

It is extremely important that you build your support network. The people you meet at or outside of work could help you land a future job which may lead to a successful career. Expand your contact. This is one of the best ways to put your name out there.

Do not forget to set your goals

It is important that you have a clear idea of what you want to build in the long term. It is equally important that you set small goals to help you get where you want to go or become who you want to be.

Set your goals. Let them guide and steer you in the right direction—the one that leads to your success and happiness.

Search for "Eckhart Tolle by Karen Harris" on Amazon to check out the rest of the book

CPSIA information can be obtained at www.ICGtesting.com
Printed in the USA
LVOW04s1412251015

459660LV00027B/1104/P